GRAINS
of
STARDUST

GRAINS of STARDUST

vismaya mohanlal

PENGUIN BOOKS

An imprint of Penguin Random House

PENGUIN BOOKS

USA | Canada | UK | Ireland | Australia
New Zealand | India | South Africa | China

Penguin Books is part of the Penguin Random House group of companies
whose addresses can be found at global.penguinrandomhouse.com

Published by Penguin Random House India Pvt. Ltd
7th Floor, Infinity Tower C, DLF Cyber City,
Gurgaon 122 002, Haryana, India

Penguin
Random House
India

First published in Penguin Books by Penguin Random House India 2021

10 9 8 7 6 5 4 3 2 1

ISBN 9780143451860

Typeset in Bembo Std by Manipal Technologies Limited, Manipal
Printed at Replika Press Pvt. Ltd, India

www.penguin.co.in

FOREWORD

'When I sit down to write, which is the essential moment in my life, I am completely alone', wrote Gabriel Garcia Marquez, the world-renowned Latin American writer. How true an affirmation! Words are born first in the mindscape. Thereafter, they flow through the pen in one's hand, assimilating one's innermost thoughts, and eventually cascade in an avalanche on to the blank paper. The radiant glow of the intellect illuminates it and touches the reader sitting in some anonymous nook. When I read the works of great scriptwriters, the actor in me experiences this immanence; the inexplicable power of words. I am able to imbibe that which the solitary writer experiences in the throes of creation, and thereby give expression to it in my own art form.

Painting too is a lonely craft, a complex and solitary endeavour. Yet, when shapes and colours fall in love under the artist's hand, the onlooker also experiences a silent eruption of intimate feeling. This I believe to be the reflective nature of art, wherein the illusory distinction between the 'I' and the 'other' is dissolved in the mirror of human experience.

I am not competent enough to speak with authority on the intricacies of a literary genre such as poetry. I seek only to relate what I make of it personally. To me, poetry is the fine balance of subtlety and eloquence. It is an undertaking that calls for deep contemplation; for access to the mysterious power of words. With the play of a few words, the great poets evoke myriad emotions in the reader. Hence the universal appeal of their poems, and their ability to transcend the boundaries of time and place.

Matsuo Basho, an exponent of the traditional Japanese haiku, is, in my opinion, a prime example of such a poet. Every line of Basho's is a sensory delight, a journey and a destination in itself. 'The journey itself is home', he insists, and I believe that the following verses by him serve as a testament to this declaration:

'The temple bell stops.
But the sound keeps coming
out of the flowers.'

'I like to wash,
The dust of this world
In the droplets of dew.'

I was reminded of Basho while reading some of Vismaya's poems. I found in them a strange expression of thought reflecting feeling more than meaning, accompanied by illustrations that reinforce the thematic content. From my understanding, this is what *Grains of Stardust* is: a synesthetic stream of consciousness that does not distinguish between journey and destination, but meanders unchecked upon the river of human emotion.

It is my hope and prayer that the vision of legendary poets like Basho will guide the words and thoughts of my daughter, and remain forever the fountainhead of her inspiration. Recalling a little poem by Basho, I sign off wishing everyone the very best.

'An old pond,
A frog jumps in—
The sound of water.'

—Mohanlal

And I'll meet you on the other side of hesitation . . .

Read my poetry out loud
Breathe it in
and taste the letters pour out.

A delicious sound.

Do you hear the colours take form?

Feel the pages move you
as you float in space

make some space

Open your mind
and get inside
and see all that
shimmering
marmalade liquid.

Grains of stardust

I FEEL THE EARTH SPINNING

I FEEL IT ALL THE TIME

A SLOW PIROUETTE

AND TODAY
I'M READY

I GET OUT MY TUTU

I PLIÉ

I LET OUT MY BREATH.

I wonder whether all the stars
that we cannot see
are hidden somewhere
within our souls?
Or if our souls
are those stars
in the night sky
And we, the reflection
of the universe.

A pencil to my heart
The lead slowly makes its way through
Willing the words to bleed

let's get these ballet fingers on point
wiggle your pencil toes
sharpen your mind and erase your fears
Focus.
breathe into your core
breathe out ink
make those letters dance

Floating underwater
Imagining I'm in space
Every cell in my body
Dancing ballet

Caterpillar eyebrows
Tomato cherry cheeks
Wiggles and giggles
I can't seem to speak

my heart he takes
one bite at a time

a delicious cake
he chews slowly

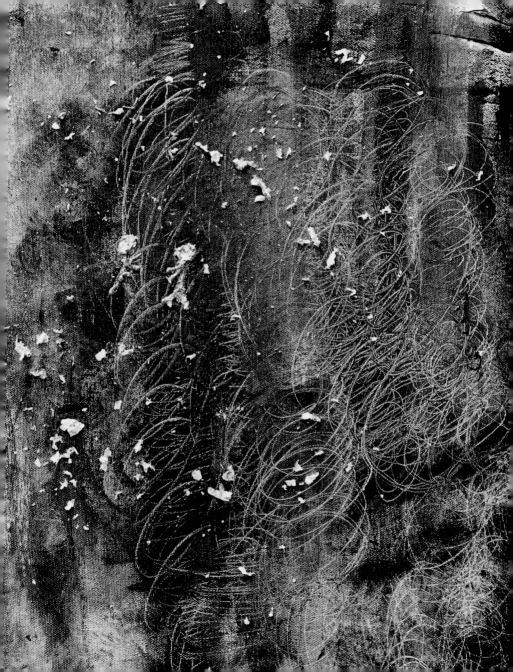

Your energy
Cool still waters
keeps me awake,
yearning to dip my toes in
I fantasize of what
we could be

you and I

swimming
through
galaxies

escape.

Grains of stardust
in a whirlwind of glitter
suspended in space
Stardust in your eyes
as they look into mine
Stardust in our souls
as our bodies entwine

twinkling and sparkling
sprinkling and spinning
We're glowing, we're flowing
we're smiling, we're vibing

And here we go again
You've got magic in your eyes
And I can't look away
But I've been fooled too many times

Insecurity, a ring stuck on my chubby finger.
I hide her well.
Scrunched up fists
Deep in my pockets.
And when you reach out to shake my hand
I look the other way
But you don't understand

I look at you
You look away
Maybe it's too late
Maybe it was a mistake

Trying to keep the candle alight
Trying to capture the spark from that night
But how can I?
When I can't even articulate
Words into sentences
Sentences into meaning
My heart races and all I can
come up with is
'Hey, how's it going?'

And of course you think
You think that to converse I need a drink
And maybe you're right

Because the courage that I had to finally talk to
    you
That courage was only there
For that one night

Figures of eights
Surrounded by fours
I wait and wait
But you never show

I throw myself into the sun
Sunlight melts my skin
Candle wax

I ask the moon what went wrong
The moon shows her face
Lights her fire

And now I understand

Wait for it.

You waited at eight
But I at seven
Tick tock tack
Till it was eleven
and I shut the gate
I was too early
And you too late

And I wonder
If only I waited an hour longer
The possibilities inflate
An empty slate
Endless.

If we decided on nine
And made it on time
What then?
Would our memories be fonder?
You and I on the same line
Hands entwined
Ponder Ponder Ponder

My eyes yours and yours mine.

Falling deeper
Little droplets of light
Swallowing my being
A joyous feeling
Falling deeper
into the depths of my soul
Love leaping her way into every single cell

My mind
An abstract painting
My thoughts
Have no beginning
Stuck somewhere in between
I move around in circles
Swimming in colours
A delicious confusion

Staring into emptiness
I see my reflection
I wear many masks

Get into your inspiration
Assess
And feel
The fibre of your being

Freeing the body
Feeling the mind

Slow but steady
Take a step before you're ready
Jump before you think.
On the count of three
Move when you're on the brink.
In those moments you'll find spontaneity
Slow and then quick.
A thought-out naivety

The beat sinks its fingers
Into my heart and starts drumming

PAT A PAT A PAT A PAT A PAT A PAT A PAT

Moving my soul
To every limb and cell
A furnace in my belly
Crackling
And I'm one with the flame

You call it dancing
I call it burning

The Dance of Consciousness

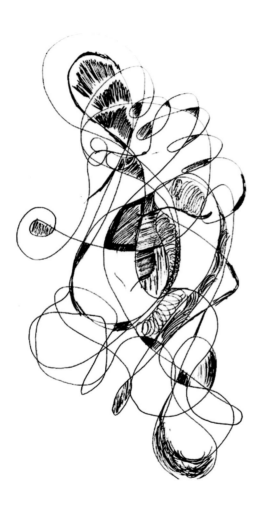

I'm thinking
of stars erupting
and galaxies forming
of molten fireballs exploding
in space
and then
you and I
breathing
in this space

And how could I let this happen again?
How could I give my heart away
When I just got it back

A hickey is what you are
A little red blotch
With its tentacles of lust
Struggling to get skin-deep;
Superficial.
I'll smother you with foundation
Keep you hidden
Because you're here one day
etched on to my neck
And gone too soon
Never long enough to stay

They think I have a play-dough heart.
When they're bored, they come make some art.
Tearing, squeezing, rolling and squishing
Pinching, Prodding
They don't hear me screaming

Clock ticking. Feet tapping. Fingers drumming.
Heavy breathing. Neck cracking. Mind spinning.
World reeling. Heart freezing. Tears rolling. Fear
    growing.
breath slowing. breath slowing.

It's happening . . .
happening so fast . . .
Happening again.

happening too soon

I can't let go.

I'm falling

falling

falling in love

falling

falling

Falling in love in the worst way.

Look away
Hold your breath
Swallow your feelings

Imagination

ODE OF AN IDLI

An idli sat idly one Saturday afternoon.
Somewhere in the middle of the bowl
Sandwiched between Iddlytum and Iddlytoo.

As usual, everyone was singing their idli worship
      song

'Oh Sambar, Oh Chamandi, Chutney, Chutney,
      Chutney.
We offer ourselves to thee.
For we are tasteless and useless without thee.
Oh glory, glory liquid.
Come make us taste good.'

This sitting idli, however, did not sing.
Why should he worship some liquid
that would supposedly add flavour to his life?
Why could he not be complete on his own?

And so, while all the others sang

This fluffy idli
rolled his eyes and stuck his tongue out.

They put me on a pedestal
And I throw my soul into a dry well

Their pseudo sparkles of laughter
Strangle my mind
As mine echoes theirs
in perfect time

Painting on mirrors
We sit and spend hours
Layers and layers
But what are we
Beneath it all?

Shatter the glass
Swallow the pieces
Bleed out your truth

Caterpillar crawling
Taking its time
Always stalling
Never acknowledging its crime.
From the tiny holes in the ground
to the minute yet monstrous atom bubbles,
The butterfly begs to be found
To get over all his troubles.

AND
WHO
AM
I ?

I come to you in waves
Like an ocean licking your face

AND `I´ FOREVER LOOKS AT
HER REFLECTION IN THE WATER

BLINDED TO THE TRUTH.

THAT SHE'S NOT JUST HER
REFLECTION

BUT THE WHOLE DAMN POND.

To completely eradicate this self to find myself
The paradox
The illusion

'I'.
A naming ceremony.

And 'I' forever looks at her reflection in the water.
Blinded to the truth
That she's not just her reflection
But the whole damn pond.

Travelling through my soul
I seek the glitter and the shine
The energy of the divine

A seeker disguised as an ignorant fool
Craving knowledge, leeching on to truth
Ears pricked and mind astute

Little pearls of goosebumps form
in a circle around my thigh
As they suck and suck and tickle
I shake in delight with an exuberant smile

This is me

There is no me

There is no I

WE
WE
WE

Grains of stardust
Exploded within the spheres of our minds

Sparkling in the sand
Our lives in our own hands

The only way
is to know
That I is not me
There is no I
There is only we

A spark in your eye
As it meets mine
A sudden warmth in my chest
And you've already caught my breath

Liquid made of sunshine
Twisting its way
up and down my spine
An ocean of dragonflies

I never taste my words before they leave my
    mouth
And before I know it,
I'm left with the aftertaste
Biting my tongue
a little too late

My thoughts stuck in a blender
Round and round it goes
Rubber wheels crushed by glass shards

A hailstorm
Thousands of sand grains
splatter on my forehead

My mind deflates
While thoughts of you
evaporate

Doubt, like creepers, entwining its
raspy fingers around my
diaphragm
Blowing explosive raspberries
on my belly rolls
Pinning me down
Unable to move
Kneading all the air out
Making flabby chapattis
I laugh uncontrollably, begging it to stop

Dear Brain, please shut up

My mind is a dog chasing its tail
A cocktail of dizziness and self-sabotage

TEQUILA

My sobs pull the worms out of my chest
How many more are hidden in there?
How many times
How many times?
I never seem to learn
A headless chicken.

'That's all in the past'
Only to be back where I began.
'Never again'
A phrase that's become a joke.
'I'll count'
'I'll talk to myself before'
But I forget
'I'm in control' says the goldfish
drowning in tequila.

And it's always the same.
It starts with a few
And before I know it,
I snap back into consciousness
Not knowing that I had even lost it.

Fear. Guilt. Shame.
Bricks upon my shoulders.

I long to escape from myself
knowing all too well now that the self
I try to escape from
is the self I become when I do escape.

I run through my brain
Flashlight in hand
But the darkness blinds my soul
A black hole.

I open my eyes and look around.
Inhale.
Gratefulness.
But how much longer till luck loses her patience?
How many times?
How many before I die?

WINE

Today I woke up in the pool
Regained consciousness
with a splash

Unsteady and drenched
A scrunched forehead
The water washing away every grain of memory.

My hippocampus fell asleep again
Turning all my memories into a forgotten dream.

Laughter, music and wine

Wine
Now synonymous with vomit.
I feel the liquid coursing through my body.
Sweet wine turned poison
Making my whole being purge

And I close my eyes and think
'Not again'

But this time
This time

There's no guilt or shame showering over me.
There aren't any drops left.
I've used it all up.

Instead in its place
A feeling that inhibits me from feeling anything
A paradox

My eyes roll back and I succumb to this numbness.

AND WHERE DO I GO?

Pineapple sunsets on the radio
Prune-coloured faces shaped like a potato
Running wild races
Round and round
Roaring loud noises
Just to feel the sound

The silence between you and I

A lullaby,
Awakening us to feel time in all its glory

DEATH IS ON HIS WAY

AND LIFE
GASPS IN
EXCITEMENT

A FIRST DATE.

Always in the clouds
My head pumps air into my mind
A vagabond balloon
drifting in circles,
whistling away the blues.

You're just some banana peel I slipped on
A mistake

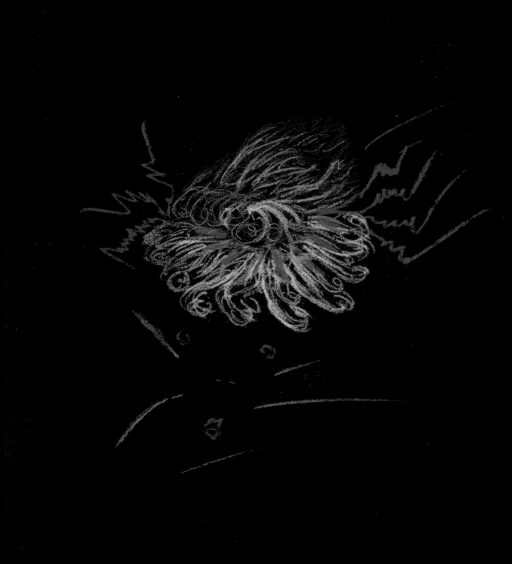

Oops!

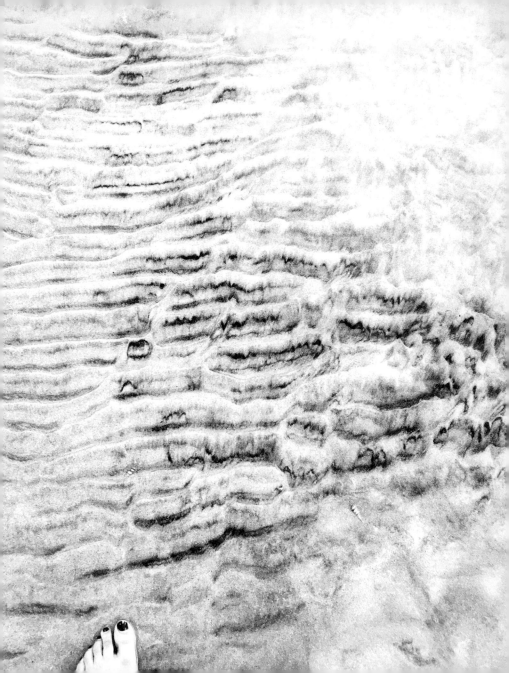

Do you ever feel
that in a moment everything could crumple
under your feet, as if it were all made of paper?
As if everything could just dissolve and disappear
And there you are.
In nothingness.

In nothingness with stars all around you.

The days turned into emerald snails
Smooth and slow they moved
And the winter brought howling whales
Swimming around my head
Tweety birds pretended to fly
In circles around the fire
The trampoline let out a cry
That he could not take them higher
'Why?' he questioned
Why lie about those sparks
When within, you possess a star?
Bright and glowing, it marked
your dying ember heart
Cowering beneath the layers of mystery
as watery as my onion eye
If your freedom stuck to you like glue
and wouldn't let you move
And if your dreams crossed that fine line
where there's an infinite sigh
Why hide
When you were born to shine?

When all the light has been sucked out
And you're a teardrop waiting to spill
hanging upside down on some broken cloud
waiting for a lightning bolt
My fire will scorch your soul
And put your mind to rest

You'll feel the tingle in your toes
As I slowly work my way up
And before you know it, you'll be laughing again
with your hair in the wind and your smile in
    the sky
your tongue flying out in freedom

You stir your paintbrush in my heart
As you empty out my kaleidoscope of emotion
The colours pouring out
You paint my feelings and thoughts
Never once expressing yours
Just playing with mine
Creating your masterpiece of chaos.

You're a mirage
A trance
A furry star

Too comfortable and bright

Chessboard
Checkmate
One move
And I'm yours
And here we are
Frozen in limbo
I, forever waiting for that blow
And you, forever keeping me there

Savouring the wondrous gushing blue
Sinking in me and I'm sinking in you

Flowing salmon of consciousness
swimming upstream
against the flow
Maybe it's time for me to let go
See where this takes me

Time is fleeting
Bring out the ships
Drenched in fire
My lips lick the flames
Come rip my heart
and set me ablaze
Sunsets and cigarettes
Cigarettes and smiles

My heart feels weak and heavy
Illusions pressing their palms
on my chest

Breathing out bubbles of infatuation and lust

Carry my heart on a sleeve I did
As the hungry beasts clawed
their nails into it

And I sweep by
trying to capture every tiny molecule
of love that has been lost

Unaware that I have it all in my pocket.

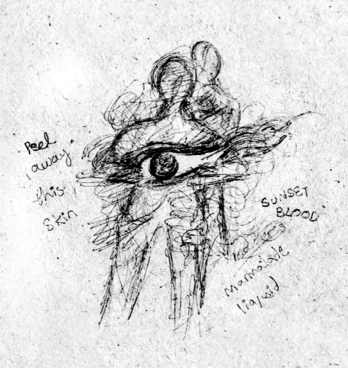

peel
away
this
skin

SUNSET
BLOOD

marmalade
liquid

a furnace in my belly
a yearning in my fingertips

To leap
To roar
Rip my chest open
and let all this light explode
Grains of stardust

A puddle
A footstep
A splash
And I'm wet
Your tie
My dress
We undress
Outside
Fireflies
A deep sigh
hearts collide
Get inside
Slow and quiet
Imagination
Anywhere
And you're right there
A sweet nightmare.

A game I no longer understand
But a puzzle I have yet to solve.
Will your hands still fit mine?

THE END PUZZLE

Where can one go?
Where can one hide?
If to find is to stay
And to leave is to search?
If there is no freedom to either?

Is it not an illusion?
A blinding light to my eyes,
cackling as I lose sight

If you're the missing puzzle piece
tucked away in the corner, under the fish bowl,
Speak!

Puzzle piece:

I am indeed the tiny puzzle piece
Living under the fish bowl
I watch Goldie day and night
to twilight and back
Round and round she goes
And I can't help but think that

'We're not that different, Goldie,
You and I
My life chained to one picture
One puzzle
I would never fit another as perfectly
as I would the one I was created for

But what if
   imperfection made perfection

The displacement, the beauty

If I was able to choose any puzzle to belong to
Only then would I be free
As you would be, if you were let out into the sea.'

BLUE BLACK BLUE BLACK BLUE
BLACK BLUE YELLOW BLACK BLUE
BLACK BLUE BLACK BLUE BLACK BLUE

I am the YELLOW
The bold YELLOW.
The brave YELLOW
The sun YELLOW.
The YELLOW that yells from
the minuscule dandelion hairs
that float in the air to the hills

We all crave freedom. We do.

Why do they choose to stay so orderly?

Washed washed wish washed
Brain washed
Scrub scrub scrubbers.
There they go again
Jibber jabber jib
Petty oh so petty
Chasing sparkles
They're all the same
Disillusioned.
Not knowing that beauty is also in the mundane

I remain YELLOW and I wait to become GREEN

So I can have a bit of you
and a bit of me
For there is no 'I'
without you.

'You're part of a bigger picture'
I was told
But could it be I was told that
Just so I would have some faith to hold?

Truth be told
We're two puzzle pieces
that would never fit.
We could try
But you'd still be you
And I'd still be I

And together our colours would combine

Another colour in your book
A hook in my heart

But I'd never be GREEN
And thus never be free

Because BLUE you're water
and I'm oil
You're sand
and I'm fire

You've told me from the start
that we have different desires.
I ignored my intuition
Thinking I could change the situation

Change. Change. Change.
The only thing that stays the same.

In the end
We're just two dice
being rolled onto a board
Twisting our bodies in hope
For that one or six
No way of knowing
But always hoping
Forever rolling
          rolling
            rolling
          till
            THE END.